THE WELSH PANTRY - Y PANTRY CYMREIG

RECIPES FROM WALES - RYSEITIAU O GYMRU

Sian Llewellyn

DOMINO BOOKS (WALES) LTD

METRIC/IMPERIAL/AMERICAN UNITS

We are all used to doubling or halving a recipe. Thus, a Victoria sandwich may be made using 4 oz each of flour, sugar and butter with 2 eggs or 6 oz each of flour, sugar and butter with 3 eggs. The proportions of the ingredients are unchanged. This must be so for all units. Use either the metric units or the imperial units given in the recipes, do not mix the two.

It is not practical to give the exact equivalents of metric and imperial units because 1 oz equals 28.35 g and 1 pint equals 568 ml. The tables on page vi indicate suitable quantities but liquids should be carefully added to obtain the correct consistency. See also the charts on page iv.

PINTS TO MILLILITRES AND LITRES
The following are approximations only

¼ pint = 150 ml
½ pint = 275 ml
¾ pint = 425 ml

1 pint = 575 ml
1¾ pints = 1000 ml (1 litre)
3 pints = 1½ litres

CONTENTS - CYNNWYS

	Page - Tudalen
Foreword - Rhagair	v
Soups - Cawl	7
Savoury Dishes - Blasusfwyd	10
Fish - Pysgod	17
Meat - Cigoedd	23
Cakes - Teisennau	29
Desserts - Pwdinau	35
Preserves and Jams - Cyffaith a Jam	39
Confectionery - Melysfwyd	42
Drinks - Diodydd	45
Units, American Equivalents - Unedau, unedau cyfwerth Americanaidd	ii, iv, vi
Index - Mynegai	47

© D C P and E J P, 1990 Reprinted 1991, 1992 (twice), 1993, 1994, 1995 (twice), 1996, 1997
Welsh translation by Delyth Evans - Cyfieithiad Cymraeg gan Delyth Evans
Cover photograph by Michael Corrin - Llun y clawr gan Michael Corrin
Illustrations by Allison Fewtrell - Darluniau gan Allison Fewtrell
ISBN 1 85772 003 2

The following charts give the approximate equivalents for metric and imperial weights, and oven temperatures.

Ounces	Approx g to nearest whole number	Approx g to nearest whole 25 g
1	28	25
2	57	50
3	85	75
4	113	125
5	142	150
6	170	175
7	198	200
8	226	225
9	255	250
10	283	275
11	311	300
12	340	350
13	368	375
14	396	400
15	428	425
16	456	450

OVEN TEMPERATURE GUIDE

	Electricity °C	°F	Gas Mark
Very cool	110	225	$\frac{1}{4}$
	130	250	$\frac{1}{2}$
Cool	140	275	1
	150	300	2
Moderate	170	325	3
	180	350	4
Moderately hot	190	375	5
	200	400	6
Hot	220	425	7
	230	450	8
Very hot	240	475	9

When using this chart for weights over 16 ounces, add the appropriate figures in the column giving the nearest whole number of grammes and then adjust to the nearest unit of 25. For example, 18 oz (16 oz + 2 oz) becomes 456 + 57 = 513 to the nearest whole number and 500 g to the nearest unit of 25.

Throughout the book, 1 teaspoon = 5 ml and 1 tablespoon = 15 ml.

FOREWORD - RHAGAIR

Traditional Welsh cooking is based on home-grown produce. Wales is mainly a pastoral country and market stalls are weighed down with Welsh butter, cheese, eggs, lamb, fish, laverbread, leeks, potatoes and other vegetables.

In keeping with today's more sedentary lifestyle and new ideas about diet, some traditional recipes have changed slightly: a little less sugar in the cakes, cawl is skimmed to remove fat and more wholemeal flour is used: but the taste and goodness of wholesome food remains.

The focal point of the Welsh kitchen was the open hearth. The main meal at the turn of the century would probably have been cawl, soup cooked in a pot suspended over the fire: meat, pork or lamb, boiled until it was tender, with home-grown vegetables and sometimes oats to thicken it. Often, the meat provided one meal and the vegetables another.

Doughs and batters were cooked on a griddle, a flat thick iron disc some 45 cm (18 inches) in diameter. Today, a thick based frying pan or saucepan is often used but Welsh cakes and Welsh pancakes with currants are just as delicious however they are cooked.

With over 750 miles of coastline and inland rivers, Wales is rich in fish. From early times, fish were pickled, cured and smoked for the winter and hams of mutton hung in the kitchen next to mackerel or herring.

Many recipes were created for special occasions, when visitors were expected or workers celebrated a task well done: harvest broth, threshing cake, shearing cake, fairing pies, tinker's cake, Llanddarog Fair cake, Michaelmas cawl, and so on. Some of these are in this book, others are in the companion books, *Country Cooking, Recipes from Wales* and *Celtic Recipes*.

A special word about laverbread. The taste for this is an acquired one and the rich and the famous often have this delicacy sent to them by special delivery. However, it does not travel well and is best cooked soon after it is bought and eaten immediately. For many living away from their homeland, it is one of the many reasons for coming back to Wales.

S L

AMERICAN MEASURES

American measures are given by volume and weight using standard cups and spoons.

US Standard Measuring Spoons and Cups

1 tablespoon = 3 teaspoons = ½ fluid ounce = 14.2 ml
2 tablespoons = 1 fluid ounce = 28 ml
4 tablespoons = ¼ cup
5 tablespoons = ⅓ cup
8 tablespoons = ½ cup
10 tablespoons = ⅔ cup
12 tablespoons = ¾ cup
16 tablespoons = 2 cups = 8 fluid ounces = ½ US pint
32 tablespoons = 2 cups = 16 fluid ounces = 1 US pint.

Metric (Imperial)	American
1 teaspoon	1 teaspoon
1 tablespoon	1 tablespoon
1½ teaspoons	2 tablespoons
2 tablespoons	3 tablespoons
3 tablespoons	¼ (scant) cup
4 tablespoons	5 tablespoons
5 tablespoons	6 tablespoons
5½ tablespoons	7 tablespoons
6 tablespoons (scant ¼ pint)	½ cup
¼ pint	⅔ cup
scant ½ pint	1 cup
½ pint (10 fl oz)	1¼ cups
¾ pint (15 fl oz)	scant 2 cups
¾ pint (16 fl oz)	2 cups (1 pint)
1 pint (20 fl oz)	2½ cups

Metric (Imperial)	American
flour, plain or self-raising	
15 g (½ oz)	2 tablespoons
25 g (1 oz)	1¼ cup
100/125 g (4 oz)	1 cup
sugar, caster or granulated, brown (firmly packed)	
25 g (1 oz)	2 tablespoons
100/125 g (4 oz)	½ cup
200/225 g (8 oz)	1 cup
butter, margarine, fat	
1 oz	2 tablespoons
225 g (8 oz)	1 cup
150 g (5 oz) shredded suet	1 cup

1 cup (American) contains approximately

100/125 g (4 oz) grated cheese, 50 g (2 oz) fresh breadcrumbs,
100 g (4 oz) dried breadcrumbs,
100/125 g (4 oz) pickled beetroot, button mushrooms, shelled peas, red/blackcurrants, 5 oz strawberries,
175 g (6 oz) raisins, currants, sultanas, chopped candied peel, stoned dates,
225 g (8 oz) glacé cherries, 150 g (5 oz) shelled whole walnuts,
100 g (4 oz) chopped nuts,
75 g (3 oz) desiccated coconut,
225 g (8 oz) cottage cheese,
100/125 g (4 oz) curry powder,
225 g (8 oz) minced raw meat,
⅜ pint (7½ fl oz) cream.

SOUPS - CAWL

LEEK AND POTATO SOUP - CAWL CENNIN A THATWS

METRIC
1 kg potatoes
3 leeks
4 tablespoons chopped chives
salt and pepper
425 ml chicken stock
425 ml milk
4 tablespoons cream

IMPERIAL
2 lb potatoes
3 leeks
4 tablespoons chopped chives
salt and pepper
¾ pint chicken stock
¾ pint milk
4 tablespoons cream

Peel and dice the potatoes. Wash and cut up the leeks including some of the green tops. Cook the potatoes and leeks in the chicken stock for 20 minutes until soft. Season. Pour into a blender and blend for a few seconds. Return to the pan and add the milk. Re-heat. Serve hot with cream and sprinkled with chopped chives.

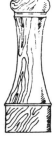

CHICKEN AND LEEK SOUP - CAWL CYW IÂR A CHENNIN

METRIC
1 small chicken
2 chicken stock cubes
2 litres water
6 leeks
salt and pepper

IMPERIAL
1 small chicken
2 chicken stock cubes
4 pints water
6 leeks
salt and pepper

Clean and joint the chicken. Dissolve the stock cubes in the water in a large pan and add the chicken. Clean and trim the leeks. Cut up including some of the green tops and add to the pan. Simmer for 3 hours. Cool and skim off the fat. Re-heat for a further 30 minutes. To serve: remove the meat from the bones and place at the bottom of individual soup bowls. Pour the hot soup over the meat.

ONION SOUP - CAWL NIONOD

METRIC
4 medium sized onions
50 g butter
1 litre milk
1 tablespoon flour
salt and pepper
4 tablespoons cream

IMPERIAL
4 medium sized onions
2 oz butter
2 pints milk
1 tablespoon flour
salt and pepper
4 tablespoons cream

Skin and very finely slice the onions. Fry in the butter until soft but not brown. Remove the pan from the heat and stir in the flour and 3 tablespoons milk. Slowly stir in the rest of the milk and season. Heat gently until the soup is smooth and creamy. If preferred, blend in a food processor for a few seconds. Serve hot with cream.

HARVEST SOUP - CAWL CYNHAEAF

METRIC	IMPERIAL
1 kg Welsh neck of lamb	2 lb Welsh neck of lamb
1 kg potatoes	2 lb potatoes
500 g leeks	1 lb leeks
500 g onions	1 lb onions
500 g carrots	1 lb carrots
1 medium sized turnip	1 medium sized turnip
salt and pepper	salt and pepper

Remove as much fat as possible from the meat. Boil in 1.5 litres (3 pints) water. Skim the surface from time to time to remove as much fat as possible. Cook for 2¼ hours. Peel and dice the vegetables and add to the meat. Season. Simmer for 10 - 15 minutes until the vegetables are cooked. Serve hot.

SAVOURY DISHES - BLASUSFWYD

EGGS AND LEEKS - WYAU A CHENNIN

METRIC
4 small leeks
15 g butter
2 eggs
2 tablespoons milk
salt and pepper

IMPERIAL
4 small leeks
½ oz butter
2 eggs
2 tablespoons milk
salt and pepper

Wash and trim the leeks. Cut up and boil in salted water for 10 - 15 minutes until soft. Drain and dot with butter and season. Beat the eggs and milk and cook as scrambled eggs in a pan. Place the leeks on a warm dish and cover with the scrambled eggs. Serve hot.

HAM, LEEKS AND CHEESE - HAM, CENNIN A CHAWS

METRIC
6 leeks
6 slices of cooked ham
50 g butter
25 g flour
100 g Cheddar cheese
500 ml milk
25 g breadcrumbs
salt and pepper

IMPERIAL
6 leeks
6 slices of cooked ham
2 oz butter
1 oz flour
4 oz Cheddar cheese
1 pint milk
1 oz breadcrumbs
salt and pepper

Wash and trim the leeks and cook in salted, boiling water for 10 - 15 minutes until soft. Drain and place on a warm dish. Melt half the butter in a pan and stir in the flour using a wooden spoon. Warm gently for 1 minute. Remove the pan from the heat and slowly add the milk, stirring to prevent the formation of lumps. Cook slowly, stirring, until the sauce thickens. Grate the cheese. Stir 75 g (3 oz) of the cheese into the sauce and season to taste. Wrap each of the leeks in a slice of ham and place in an ovenproof dish. Pour over the sauce. Mix the breadcrumbs and remaining cheese and sprinkle over the sauce. Dot with butter. Place the dish under the grill until the breadcrumbs and cheese are golden.

LAVERBREAD AND BACON - BARA LAWR A CHIG MOCH

METRIC
200 g prepared laverbread*
6 rashers bacon

IMPERIAL
8 oz prepared laverbread*
6 rashers bacon

Buy the laverbread from the market coated with oatmeal (optional). Fry the bacon and remove to a warm dish. Using a spoon, form the laverbread into cakes and cook in the bacon fat for 4 - 5 minutes until thoroughly cooked through. Serve bacon and laverbread hot.

*The laverbread bought in the shops and markets has already been washed and boiled for several hours. It is ready for frying and is sold with or without oatmeal.

WELSH RAREBIT - CAWS POB

METRIC
4 slices hot buttered toast
200 g grated Cheddar cheese
25 g butter
1 teaspoon dry mustard
3 tablespoons milk
3 drops Worcestershire sauce
salt and pepper

IMPERIAL
4 slices hot buttered toast
8 oz grated Cheddar cheese
1 oz butter
1 teaspoon dry mustard
3 tablespoons milk
3 drops Worcestershire sauce
salt and pepper

Melt the butter in a saucepan. Stir in the remaining ingredients and warm gently. Pour over the toast and serve hot.

BUCK RAREBIT - CAWS POB A WY

Make the toast and cheese mixture as for Welsh rarebit. Top each slice with a poached egg.

FAGGOTS AND PEAS - FFAGOTS A PHYS

METRIC	IMPERIAL
500 g pig's liver	1 lb pig's liver
250 g breadcrumbs	8 oz breadcrumbs
500 g onions	1 lb onions
50 g butter or pork fat	2 oz butter or pork fat
1 teaspoon dried sage	1 teaspoon dried sage
Gravy	**Gravy**
1 tablespoon flour	1 tablespoon flour
600 ml water	1 pint water

Soak the liver in boiling water for a few minutes then remove from the water and mince. Skin and chop the onions. Mix all the ingredients together and turn into a greased 20 cm (8 inch) square meat tin. Cook in a moderately hot oven (200°C, 400°F, gas mark 6) for 20 minutes. Cut into squares and remove to a hot dish.

Gravy: Add the flour to the meat tin and work into a smooth paste. Stir in 600 ml (1 pint) water. Heat until the gravy boils. Serve the faggots with boiled potatoes, green peas and the gravy.

GLAMORGAN SAUSAGES - SELSIG MORGANNWG

METRIC
150 g breadcrumbs
75 g Cheddar cheese
1 small onion
25 g butter
pinch dry mustard
pinch mixed herbs
2 tablespoons flour
1 egg

IMPERIAL
6 oz breadcrumbs
3 oz Cheddar cheese
1 small onion
1 oz butter
pinch dry mustard
pinch mixed herbs
2 tablespoons flour
1 egg

Grate the cheese. Skin and cut up the onion and fry in the butter until it has softened. Mix the cheese, onion and breadcrumbs together. Season with the herbs and mustard. Separate the egg. Use the yolk to bind the mixture. Form into small sausages and roll in flour. Deep fry.

CAERPHILLY PUDDING - PWDIN CAERFFILI

METRIC
50 g grated Caerphilly cheese
50 g breadcrumbs
25 g butter
250 ml milk
2 eggs
pinch salt

IMPERIAL
2 oz grated Caerphilly cheese
2 oz breadcrumbs
1 oz butter
½ pint milk
2 eggs
pinch salt

SAVOURY DISHES - BLASUSFWYD

Mix half the cheese with the breadcrumbs. Season. Melt the butter in the milk. Separate the eggs and lightly beat the yolk. Add the milk and butter and eggs to the cheese mixture. Bake in a moderate oven (170°C, 325°F, gas mark 3) for 30 minutes. Whip the egg whites until stiff. Spread over the pudding, sprinkle with the rest of the cheese and return to the oven until browned.

POTATO CAKES - TEISENNAU TATWS

METRIC	IMPERIAL
400 g potatoes	1 lb potatoes
25 g butter	1 oz butter
2 tablespoons milk	2 tablespoons milk
100 g grated Cheddar cheese	4 oz grated Cheddar cheese
1 tablespoon chopped chives	1 tablespoon chopped chives
salt and pepper	salt and pepper
flour	flour
Coating	**Coating**
100 g breadcrumbs	4 oz breadcrumbs
fat for frying	fat for frying

Boil and mash the potatoes with the butter and milk. Add the cheese and chives. Season. Allow to cool and turn on to a lightly floured board. Form into cakes. Coat with breadcrumbs and fry until golden brown.

ONION TART - TARTEN WINWNS

METRIC
Pastry
75 g margarine
150 g flour
3 tablespoons chilled water
Filling
500 g onions
25 g fat
1 tablespoon flour
450 ml cream
1 teaspoon lemon juice
salt, pepper, nutmeg

IMPERIAL
Pastry
3 oz margarine
6 oz flour
3 tablespoons chilled water
Filling
1 lb onions
1 oz fat
1 tablespoon flour
¾ pint cream
1 teaspoon lemon juice
salt, pepper, nutmeg

Pastry: Rub the margarine into the flour until the mixture looks like breadcrumbs. Add enough water, a little at a time, to make a soft dough. Line a 20 cm (8 inch) tart dish with the pastry.

Filling: Skin and thinly slice the onions. Heat gently in the fat for 20 minutes until they are soft but do not brown. Remove the pan from the heat and sprinkle the flour over the onions and stir in. Heat gently for 2 minutes. Turn the onion mixture into the tart. Add the lemon juice to the cream and season lightly. Pour over the onions. Cook in a moderately hot oven (200°C, 400°F, gas mark 6) for 25 - 30 minutes. Serve hot.

FISH - PYSGOD

PRAWN PÂTÉ - PÂTÉ CORGIMWCH

METRIC
200 g peeled prawns
75 g butter
2 teaspoons lemon juice
4 teaspoons chopped parsley
salt and pepper

IMPERIAL
8 oz peeled prawns
3 oz butter
2 teaspoons lemon juice
4 teaspoons chopped parsley
salt and pepper

Finely chop the prawns. Soften the butter. Beat the prawns into 50 g (2 oz) of the butter with the lemon juice, parsley and season. Turn into a serving dish and level. Melt the remaining butter and pour over the pâté. Chill in the refrigerator for 1 hour. Garnish with whole prawns and lemon slices. Serve with toast or French bread.

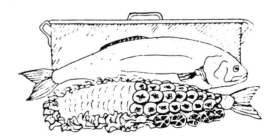

COCKLES PENCLAWDD - COCOS PENCLAWDD

METRIC
10 cockles
50 g breadcrumbs
5 spring onions
50 g butter
salt and pepper
parsley

IMPERIAL
10 cockles
2 oz breadcrumbs
5 spring onions
2 oz butter
salt and pepper
parsley

To prepare the cockles: rinse the cockles well under running water and leave to soak in cold water for 2 - 3 hours. Place the cockles in a saucepan and cover with water. Heat for about 5 minutes until the shells open. Remove the cockles from their shells and cook in fresh water for a further 4 minutes.
Melt the butter in a frying pan and add the breadcrumbs and mix. Cut up the spring onions and add to the pan. Remove the cockles from the water and shake off as much water as possible. Add the cockles to the pan. Season. Stir and heat through thoroughly. Serve sprinkled with chopped parsley.

The cockles may also be prepared as above, seasoned and served with brown bread and butter.

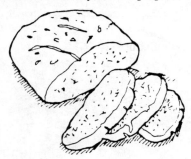

COCKLE AND BACON PIE - PASTAI COCOS A CHIG MOCH

METRIC	IMPERIAL
500 g cockles	*1 lb cockles*
6 rashers smoked bacon	*6 rashers smoked bacon*
1 large onion	*1 large onion*
50 g butter	*2 oz butter*
2 tablespoons flour	*2 tablespoons flour*
600 ml milk	*1 pint milk*
2 tablespoons chopped chives	*2 tablespoons chopped chives*
125 ml white wine	*¼ pint white wine*
salt and pepper	*salt and pepper*
Topping	**Topping**
500 g potatoes	*1 lb potatoes*
25 g butter	*1 oz butter*
50 g grated Cheddar cheese	*2 oz grated Cheddar cheese*

Prepare the cockles as in the recipe for cockles Penclawdd. Skin and chop the onion. Fry the bacon and onion in the butter in a large saucepan for 5 minutes. Remove from the heat and stir in the flour and the the milk. Re-heat stirring continuously to prevent the formation of lumps. Add the cockles, chives and white wine. Season. Simmer for 10 minutes.

Topping: Peel and boil the potatoes. Mash with butter and spread over the cockle mixture. Sprinkle with grated Cheddar cheese and bake in a moderate oven (180°C, 350°F, gas mark 4) for 30 minutes until the top is golden brown.

TEIFI SALMON - EOG TEIFI

METRIC
1 salmon
25 g butter
salt and pepper
glass of port

IMPERIAL
1 salmon
1 oz butter
salt and pepper
glass of port

Clean and prepare the fish. Brush a piece of baking foil with butter. Place the fish in the centre of the foil and dot with butter. Season lightly and pour over the glass of port. Wrap the fish in the foil and place on a baking sheet. Cook in a cool oven (150°C, 300°F, gas mark 2) allowing 10 minutes per 400 g (8 minutes per lb). Leave the salmon in the foil for 10 minutes if it is to be served hot. Remove the skin while still warm. Serve garnished with slices of cucumber and lemon.

TROUT WITH BACON - BRITHYLL A CHIG MOCH

METRIC
trout
1 rasher of bacon for each trout

IMPERIAL
trout
1 rasher of bacon for each trout

Clean and prepare the fish. Wrap each fish in a rasher of bacon and secure with a cocktail stick. Grill under a moderate heat until the bacon is crisp on one side. Turn and cook the other side. (Also delicious when grilled outdoors on a barbecue.)

FISHERMAN'S PIE - PASTAI PYSGOTWR

METRIC	IMPERIAL
400 g white fish	1 lb white fish
400 ml milk	¾ pint milk
1 bay leaf	1 bay leaf
1 slice of onion	1 slice of onion
25 g flour	1 oz flour
25 g butter	1 oz butter
50 g grated Cheddar cheese	2 oz grated Cheddar cheese
salt and pepper	salt and pepper
Topping	**Topping**
400 g potatoes	1 lb potatoes
25 g butter	1 oz butter
1 tablespoon milk	1 tablespoon milk
25 g grated Cheddar cheese	1 oz grated Cheddar cheese

Fillet the fish, taking care to remove all bones. Place in an ovenproof dish with the milk, bay leaf and onion. Season. Cover and bake in a moderate oven (180°C, 350°F, gas mark 4) for 20 minutes until the fish is cooked and flakes easily. Remove the fish and flake using a fork. Melt the butter in a pan. Remove the pan from the heat and stir in the flour using a wooden spoon. Slowly add the strained milk and juices from the fish to the pan, stirring to prevent the formation of lumps. Heat gently and cook for 2 minutes. Stir the grated cheese into the sauce. Add the flaked fish to the sauce and mix. Return the mixture to the oven proof dish.

Topping: Cook the potatoes and mash with the butter and milk. Spread over the fish. Sprinkle with cheese and bake in a moderately hot oven (200°C, 400°F, gas mark 6) for 10 - 15 minutes until golden brown.

BAKED TROUT - BRITHYLL POB

METRIC
trout
oatmeal
1 teaspoon chopped chives per trout
pinch salt
bacon dripping

IMPERIAL
trout
oatmeal
1 teaspoon chopped chives per trout
pinch salt
bacon dripping

Clean and prepare the fish. Mix the salt with the oatmeal. Coat the fish with oatmeal and place in a baking dish. Melt the fat and pour over the fish. Place the chives on top of the fish. Cover with foil and bake in a moderately hot oven (190°C, 375°F, gas mark 5) for 30 minutes. Remove the foil and leave the fish to cook for a further ten minutes to brown. Serve with green salad and brown bread.

FISH CAKES - TEISENNAU PYSGOD

METRIC
400 g cooked white fish
25 g breadcrumbs
25 g butter
1 tablespoon chopped parsley
2 tablespoons milk
Coating
100 g breadcrumbs
fat for frying

IMPERIAL
1 lb cooked white fish
1 oz breadcrumbs
1 oz butter
1 tablespoon chopped parsley
2 tablespoons milk
Coating
4 oz breadcrumbs
fat for frying

Flake the fish, taking care to remove all bones. Mix with the breadcrumbs, butter and parsley. Bind together with the milk. Form into cakes and coat with breadcrumbs. Fry in a little fat until crisp and golden.

MEAT - CIGOEDD

BIDDING PIE - PASTAI NEITHIOR

METRIC
Hot water pastry
400 g plain flour
100 g lard or chopped suet
2 teaspoons salt
250 ml water
Filling
200 g mutton
1 small onion
1 teaspoon mixed herbs
250 ml mutton stock

IMPERIAL
Hot water pastry
1 lb flour
4 oz lard or chopped suet
2 teaspoons salt
½ pint water
Filling
8 oz mutton
1 small onion
1 teaspoon mixed herbs
½ pint mutton stock

Pastry: Sift the flour and salt together. Warm the lard in the water until it melts. Make a hole in the middle of the flour and pour in the fat and water. Beat the mixture to a soft dough. Form into a ball and knead lightly. Cover with cling film or a damp towel and leave to rest for 20 - 30 minutes. Keep warm until used because the pastry becomes brittle when cold.

Bone, dice and boil the mutton. Skin and cut up the onion. Roll out half the pastry and line a greased pie dish. Place the meat and onion in the dish. Add the stock. Roll out the remaining pastry and cover the pie. Cook in a hot oven (220°C, 425°F, gas mark 7) for 20 minutes and then reduce to moderately hot (190°C, 375°F, gas mark 5) for 30 minutes.

KATT PIE - PASTAI KATT

METRIC
250 g mutton
250 g currants
250 g brown sugar
salt and pepper

IMPERIAL
8 oz mutton
8 oz currants
8 oz brown sugar
salt and pepper

Make hot water pastry as for bidding pie and line 4 greased 10 cm (4 inch) pie dishes. Mince the meat. Fill the pies with meat, adding the currants and sugar to each layer. Season. Cover with pastry lids and cook in a hot oven (220°C, 425°F, gas mark 7) for 30 minutes. Serve hot.

BACON PIE - PASTAI CIG MOCH

METRIC
Pastry
100 g margarine
200 g flour
1 tablespoon chilled water
Filling
5 rashers of lean bacon
2 small onions
15 g butter
salt and pepper

IMPERIAL
Pastry
4 oz margarine
8 oz flour
1 tablespoon chilled water
Filling
5 rashers of lean bacon
2 small onions
½ oz butter
salt and pepper

Pastry: Rub the margarine into the flour until the mixture looks like breadcrumbs. Add enough water, a little at a

time, to make a soft dough. Roll out two thirds of the pastry and line a 20 cm (8 inch) pie dish.
Filling: Cut the bacon into pieces and place on the pastry. Skin and cut up the onions. Place on top of the bacon. Season and dot with butter. Roll out the remaining pastry and cover the pie. Bake in a moderately hot oven (200°C, 400°F, gas mark 6) for 25 - 30 minutes. Serve hot.

PORK AND APPLE POTATO PIE - PASTAI PORC, AFAL A THATWS

METRIC
1 kg lean pork
2 large cooking apples
1 large onion
4 tablespoons cider or water
1 teaspoon dried sage
1 teaspoon dry mustard
salt and pepper
500 g potatoes
2 tablespoons milk
1 egg
25 g butter

IMPERIAL
2 lb lean pork
2 large cooking apples
1 large onion
4 tablespoons cider or water
1 teaspoon dried sage
1 teaspoon dry mustard
salt and pepper
1 lb potatoes
2 tablespoons milk
1 egg
1 oz butter

Cut the pork into small pieces and place in a casserole dish. Add the mustard, sage, and salt and pepper to taste. Peel and slice the apple. Skin and chop the onion. Add the apple and onion to the meat. Pour over the water or cider. Cover the casserole and cook in a moderate oven (180°C, 350°F, gas mark 4) for 1 - 1½ hours. Cook the potatoes and mash with the butter, milk and beaten egg. Remove the lid from the casserole and spread the potatoes over the meat. Return to the oven and cook for 20 minutes. Serve hot with mixed vegetables.

PHEASANT WITH PORT - FFESANT Â PHORT

METRIC
2 pheasants
25 g butter
250 ml chicken stock
6 tablespoons port
2 oranges
50 g sultanas
salt and pepper
1 tablespoon cornflour
2 tablespoons water
25 g flaked, toasted almonds

IMPERIAL
2 pheasants
1 oz butter
½ pint chicken stock
6 tablespoons port
2 oranges
2 oz sultanas
salt and pepper
1 tablespoon cornflour
2 tablespoons water
1 oz flaked, toasted almonds.

Clean and wipe the pheasants. Heat the butter in a casserole and add the pheasants. Brown all over. Pour the stock and port over the birds. Squeeze the orange and finely grate the rind. Add the strained juice, rind and sultanas to the birds. Season. Bring to the boil. Cover and cook in a moderate oven (170°C, 325°F, gas mark 3) for 1 - 1 ¼ hours. Remove the birds from the casserole and joint. Place on a warm dish. Mix the cornflour with the water and stir into the liquor in the casserole dish. Bring to the boil, stirring all the time. Pour over the pheasants and garnish with toasted almonds.

To make chicken stock, see page 27

CHICKEN STOCK - ISGELL CYW IÂR

METRIC	IMPERIAL
chicken bones	chicken bones
1 onion	1 onion
1 carrot	1 carrot
1 celery stick	1 celery stick
1 bay leaf	1 bay leaf

Place the bones in a large saucepan with 2 litres (4 pints) water. Peel and slice the onion and carrot. Clean and cut up the celery stick. Add the vegetables and bay leaf to the chicken. Bring to the boil and simmer for 3 hours. Strain the stock and allow to cool. Remove all fat from the surface.

HONEYED WELSH LAMB - CIG OEN CYMREIG A MÊL

METRIC	IMPERIAL
2 kg joint of lamb	4 lb joint of lamb
1 teaspoon ground ginger	1 teaspoon ground ginger
2 teaspoons dried rosemary	2 teaspoons dried rosemary
2 tablespoons runny honey	2 tablespoons runny honey
250 ml cider	½ pint cider
salt and pepper	salt and pepper

Rub salt, pepper and ginger all over the joint and place in a meat tin. Coat the meat with honey and sprinkle with rosemary. Pour cider around the joint. Bake in a moderately hot oven (200°C, 400°F, gas mark 6) for 30 minutes. Reduce heat to moderate (180°C, 350°F, gas mark 4) allowing a total cooking time of 30 minutes per 500 gm (per lb). Baste every 20 minutes and add more cider if needed.

WELSH SALT DUCK - HWYADEN HALLT GYMREIG

METRIC
1 duck
150 g salt
400 g small onions
25 g flour
25 g butter
450 ml milk
salt and pepper

IMPERIAL
1 duck
6 oz salt
1 lb small onions
1 oz flour
1 oz butter
¾ pint milk
salt and pepper

Rub the duck all over with salt and leave in a cool place, covered with a cloth, for a day. Turn the duck at least twice during the day. Next day, rinse the duck well and place in a large saucepan. Cover with water. Simmer slowly for 1½ - 2 hours. Skin and boil the onions in the milk until soft. Melt the butter and stir in the flour and add to the milk and onions. Season and heat gently for 2 minutes, stirring all the time to keep the liquid smooth. Drain the duck and place on a large dish. Pour the onion mixture over the duck. Serve with mixed vegetables.

CAKES - TEISENNAU

COUNTRY CAKE - CACEN FFRWYTHAU CYMYSG

METRIC	IMPERIAL
100 g plain flour	4 oz plain flour
125 g wholewheat flour	5 oz wholewheat flour
2 teaspoons baking powder	2 teaspoons baking powder
1 teaspoon mixed spice	1 teaspoon mixed spice
½ teaspoon cinnamon	½ teaspoon cinnamon
pinch salt	pinch salt
100 g soft brown sugar	4 oz soft brown sugar
100 g butter	4 oz butter
200 g mixed dried fruit	8 oz mixed dried fruit
50 g mixed chopped peel	2 oz mixed chopped peel
2 tablespoons marmalade	2 tablespoons marmalade
2 eggs	2 eggs
1 tablespoon milk	1 tablespoon milk

Sift the plain flour, baking powder, mixed spice and cinnamon together. Stir in the wholewheat flour. Rub in the butter. Stir in the remaining dry ingredients. Beat the eggs and add to the mixture with the milk. Stir in the marmalade. Turn into a greased, lined 20 cm (8 inch) round cake tin and bake in a moderate oven (170°C, 325°F, gas mark 3) for 1¼ hours. Cover the top with greased greaseproof paper if it starts to brown too much before the cake is cooked. Remove from the tin and place on a wire tray to cool.

HONEY CAKE - CACEN FÊL

METRIC
275 g plain flour
2 teaspoons baking powder
200 g butter
300 g thin honey
4 eggs
1 tablespoon lemon juice
1 teaspoon grated lemon rind
100 g chopped mixed peel
75 g chopped nuts

IMPERIAL
11 oz plain flour
2 teaspoons baking powder
8 oz butter
12 oz thin honey
4 eggs
1 tablespoon lemon juice
1 teaspoon grated lemon rind
4 oz chopped mixed peel
3 oz chopped nuts

Sift the flour and baking powder together. Cream the butter with the honey. Beat the eggs and add with the lemon juice and rind to the honey and butter. Mix well. Work in the flour. Mix in the candied peel and nuts. Turn into a large loaf tin, greased and lined with greased greaseproof paper. Bake in a moderate oven (180°C, 350°F, gas mark 4) for 1 hour.

BANANA AND HONEY TEABREAD - TORTH DE BANANA A MEL

METRIC
400 g bananas
200 g self raising flour
100 g margarine
100 g caster sugar
¼ teaspoon salt
¼ teaspoon grated nutmeg
grated rind of 1 lemon
2 eggs
8 tablespoons thick honey
6 sugar lumps

IMPERIAL
1 lb bananas
8 oz self raising flour
4 oz margarine
4 oz caster sugar
¼ teaspoon salt
¼ teaspoon grated nutmeg
grated rind of 1 lemon
2 eggs
8 tablespoons thick honey
6 sugar lumps

Sift the flour, salt and nutmeg together. Rub in the fat until the mixture looks like breadcrumbs. Stir in the sugar and lemon rind. Lightly beat the eggs. Peel and mash the bananas. Add the eggs, bananas and 6 tablespoons of the honey to the flour mixture and beat until well mixed. Turn into a greased, lined loaf tin 20 x 13 cm (8 x 5 inch) and bake in a moderate oven (180°C, 350°F, gas mark 4) for 1¼ hours until firm. Cool slightly before turning out on to a wire rack. Warm the remaining honey and spread over the top of the loaf. Roughly crush the sugar lumps and press into the honey.

CURRANT BREAD - BARA BRITH

METRIC
400 g dried, mixed fruit
250 ml strained tea
2 tablespoons marmalade
1 beaten egg
6 tablespoons brown sugar
1 teaspoon mixed spice
400 g self raising flour
1 tablespoon honey

IMPERIAL
1 lb dried, mixed fruit
½ pint strained tea
2 tablespoons marmalade
1 beaten egg
6 tablespoons brown sugar
1 teaspoon mixed spice
1 lb self raising flour
1 tablespoon honey

Soak the fruit in the tea overnight. The next day, add the marmalade, egg, sugar, spice and flour to the fruit. Mix well. Turn into a greased loaf tin and bake in a moderate oven (170°C, 325°F, gas mark 3) for 1¾ hours until firm. If the top starts to burn before the loaf is cooked, cover with a sheet of greaseproof paper. Leave in the tin for 5 minutes then tip out and stand on a wire tray. Brush the top with honey. Serve sliced and buttered. Also delicious toasted.

DATE AND WALNUT LOAF - TORTH DATYS A CHNAU FFRENGIG

METRIC
200 g stoned, chopped dates
1 teaspoon bicarbonate of soda
200 ml hot water
100 g soft brown sugar
75 g butter
200 g self raising flour

IMPERIAL
8 oz stoned, chopped dates
1 teaspoon bicarbonate of soda
½ pint hot water
4 oz soft brown sugar
3 oz butter
8 oz self raising flour

METRIC	IMPERIAL
pinch of salt	pinch of salt
1 egg	1 egg
50 g chopped walnuts	2 oz chopped walnuts

Place the dates, bicarbonate of soda and salt in a bowl. Pour over the hot water and leave to cool. Sift the flour. Rub in the butter and stir in the sugar and walnuts. Add the dry ingredients to the cooled date mixture. Beat the egg and add to make a thick batter. Turn into a greased 1kg (2 lb) loaf tin and bake in a moderate oven (180°C, 350°F, gas mark 4) for 1 - 1¼ hours until firm. Cool in the tin for 10 minutes then turn out and cool on a wire rack. Serve sliced and buttered.

PLATE CAKE - TEISEN LAP

METRIC	IMPERIAL
400 g plain flour	1 lb plain flour
100 g butter	4 oz butter
100 g lard	4 oz lard
100 g brown sugar	4 oz brown sugar
50 g currants	2 oz currants
2 eggs	2 eggs
½ teaspoon nutmeg	½ teaspoon nutmeg
milk	milk

Rub the fat into the flour until the mixture looks like breadcrumbs. Stir in the other dry ingredients. Beat the eggs. Make a hole in the middle of the cake mixture and pour in the eggs. Beat with a wooden spoon. Add enough milk to make a soft, moist mixture that drops from the spoon. Turn into a pie plate or a shallow baking tin and cook in a moderately hot oven (170°C, 325°F, gas mark 3) for 45 minutes until firm to the touch and cooked through.

WELSH CAKES - PICAU AR Y MAEN

METRIC
200 g flour
100 g butter
75 g caster sugar
50 g currants
1 teaspoon baking powder
¼ teaspoon mixed spice
2 tablespoons milk
1 egg

IMPERIAL
8 oz flour
4 oz butter
3 oz caster sugar
2 oz currants
1 teaspoon baking powder
¼ teaspoon mixed spice
2 tablespoons milk
1 egg

Sift the flour, spice and baking powder together. Rub in the butter until the mixture looks like breadcrumbs. Stir in the sugar and currants. Beat the egg and add with the milk to make a firm dough. Turn on to a floured board and roll out to a thickness of 6 mm (¼ inch). Cook on a greased griddle or thick frying pan until golden brown on both sides. Serve hot or cold, plain or buttered.

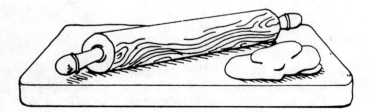

DESSERTS - PWDINAU

WATKIN WYNNE PUDDING - PWDIN WATCYN WYNNE

METRIC	IMPERIAL
200 g breadcrumbs	8 oz breadcrumbs
100 g chopped suet	4 oz chopped suet
50 g sugar	2 oz sugar
1 lemon	1 lemon
2 eggs	2 eggs
Sauce	**Sauce**
2 egg yolks	2 egg yolks
3 tablespoons sugar	3 tablespoons sugar
1 tablespoon sherry or rum or whisky	1 tablespoon sherry or rum or whisky
4 tablespoons single cream	4 tablespoons single cream

Pudding: Squeeze the lemon and strain the lemon juice. Grate the lemon rind. Mix all the dry ingredients together. Separate the eggs. Beat the egg yolks and add with the lemon juice to the dry ingredients. Beat the egg whites until stiff and fold into the pudding mxture. Turn into a pudding basin and press down gently and boil for 2 hours.
Sauce: This should be served hot and should be made just before the pudding is served. Mix all the ingredients together in a basin standing over a pan of hot water. Whisk until the sauce is pale and frothy and thick and creamy. Pour the hot sauce over individual portions of pudding.

BREAD AND BUTTER PUDDING - PWDIN BARA MENYN

METRIC
6 thin slices of bread
50 g butter
50 g sultanas/currants
2 tablespoons white or demerara sugar
1 egg
500 ml milk
½ teaspoon grated nutmeg

IMPERIAL
6 thin slices of bread
2 oz butter
2 oz sultanas/currants
2 tablespoons white or demerara sugar
1 egg
1 pint milk
½ teaspoon grated nutmeg

Butter the bread. Place a slice of the bread in an ovenproof dish and cover with the fruit and sugar. Repeat until all the bread, fruit and sugar are used up. Beat the egg and add to the milk. Strain the liquid over the bread. Leave to stand for 30 minutes. Sprinkle with a little nutmeg and bake in a moderate oven (170°C, 325°F, gas mark 3) for 45 minutes until the top is crisp and golden.

EVE'S PUDDING - PWDIN EFA

METRIC
400 g cooking apples
75 g demerara sugar
75 g margarine
75 g caster sugar
125 g self raising flour
1 egg
grated rind of 1 lemon
1 tablespoon milk

IMPERIAL
1 lb cooking apples
3 oz demerara sugar
3 oz margarine
3 oz caster sugar
5 oz self raising flour
1 egg
grated rind of 1 lemon
1 tablespoon milk

Peel and core the apples. Slice the apples and place in a greased ovenproof dish. Sprinkle the apple slices with lemon rind and demerara sugar. Cream the fat and caster sugar together until light and fluffy. Add the egg and beat well. Fold in the flour with enough milk to give a dropping consistency and spread over the apples. Bake in a moderate oven (180°C, 350°F, gas mark 4) for 45 minutes until the top is set and the sponge is golden brown and firm to the touch.

RASPBERRY ICE - SORBET MAFON

METRIC	IMPERIAL
200 g raspberries	*8 oz raspberries*
100 g caster sugar	*4 oz caster sugar*
300 ml water	*½ pint water*
juice of ½ lemon	*juice of ½ lemon*
2 egg whites	*2 egg whites*

Heat the sugar in the water in a saucepan until the sugar dissolves. Bring to the boil. Add the lemon juice and simmer gently for 10 minutes. Leave to cool. Wash and hull the raspberries. Purée the raspberries in a blender or through a sieve. When the sugar syrup is cool, stir in the raspberries. Pour into a shallow tin and freeze until mushy. (Turn the setting of the refrigerator to its lowest setting.) Beat the egg whites until stiff and fold into the mushy mixture. Return to the refrigerator. Stir occasionally and freeze until firm.

CHOCOLATE CREAMS - PWDIN SIOCLED HUFENNOG

METRIC
100 g plain chocolate
75 g unsalted butter
75 g caster sugar
3 eggs
2 teaspoons orange rind
125 ml whipping cream

IMPERIAL
4 oz plain chocolate
3 oz unsalted butter
3 oz caster sugar
3 eggs
2 teaspoons orange rind
¼ pint whipping cream

Break the chocolate into small pieces and melt in a basin standing over hot water. Remove the basin from the heat and stir in the butter and sugar. Separate the eggs. Add the egg yolks, one at a time, to the chocolate mixture. Beat well after each addition. Add the grated orange rind. Whisk the egg whites until stiff and fold into the chocolate mixture. Pour into individual dishes and put in the refrigerator to chill. Serve decorated with whipped cream.

PRESERVES AND JAMS - CYFFAITH A JAM

PLUM CHUTNEY - SHWTNI EIRIN

METRIC	IMPERIAL
1 kg plums	*2¼ lb plums*
450 g onions	*1 lb onions*
900 g cooking apples	*2 lb cooking apples*
450 g soft brown sugar	*1 lb soft brown sugar*
600 ml cider vinegar	*1 pint cider vinegar*
piece root ginger	*piece root ginger*
2 teaspoons each whole cloves, whole allspice berries and black peppercorns	*2 teaspoons each whole cloves, whole allspice berries and black peppercorns*
3 teaspoons salt	*3 teaspoons salt*

Wipe, stone and halve the plums. Skin and finely chop the onions and boil in a little water for 5 minutes to soften them. Peel, core and chop the apples. Put in a large pan with half the vinegar and cook for 20 minutes until they are a soft pulp. Bruise the ginger by hitting it with a bottle. Tie it with the other spices in a piece of muslin. Put the muslin bag of spices with the remaining vinegar and sugar into another pan. Bring to the boil and simmer for 5 minutes. Remove from the heat and leave to stand for 30 minutes. Remove the muslin bag. Add the spiced vinegar, onions, plums and salt to the apples. Bring to the boil and simmer for 2 hours until the chutney is dark and thick. Stir frequently to avoid burning. Turn into sterilized pots and seal. Leave to mature for 4 weeks before using.

CHUNKY MARMALADE - MARMALED BRAS

METRIC
1.5 kg Seville oranges
2 lemons
3.5 litres water
2.7 kg sugar

IMPERIAL
3 lb Seville oranges
2 lemons
6 pints water
6 lb sugar

Wash the oranges. Halve and squeeze out the juice and pips. Tie the pips and any membrane in a muslin bag. Squeeze the juice from the lemons. Cut the orange peel into thick slices and place in a preserving pan with the fruit juices, water and muslin bag. Simmer for 2 hours until the peel is soft and the volume of the liquid is reduced by half. Add the sugar and stir until it has dissoved. Boil rapidly for 15 minutes. When the setting point is reached remove the pan from the heat. Skim any scum from the surface. Leave to stand for 15 minutes. Pot in warm sterilized jars and seal. (To test for a set: place a small teaspoonful of the preserve on a cold saucer, cool for 20 seconds, then run a finger through it. If it wrinkles at the edges and stays in two separate sections, it is ready.)

RASPBERRY AND RHUBARB JAM - JAM MAFON A RIWBOB

METRIC
500 g rhubarb
500 g raspberries
1 kg sugar
150 ml water

IMPERIAL
1 lb rhubarb
1 lb raspberries
2 lb sugar
¼ pint water

Remove and discard the leaves of the rhubarb and trim the root. Wash and cut the stalks into pieces. Place with the water in a pan and heat until the rhubarb softens. Add the raspberries and bring to the boil. Cook for 5 minutes. Add the sugar and stir. Boil rapidly for 10 minutes until setting point is reached. (See recipe for chunky marmalade.) Leave to cool for 15 minutes then pot in warm sterilized jars and seal.

MARROW CHUTNEY - SHWTNI MARRO

METRIC	IMPERIAL
1 medium sized marrow	*1 medium sized marrow*
1 cauliflower	*1 cauliflower*
1 cucumber	*1 cucumber*
2 carrots	*2 carrots*
2 onions	*2 onions*
250 g salt	*10 oz salt*
2 litres water	*4 pints water*
Sauce	**Sauce**
75 g flour	*3 oz flour*
1 teaspoon curry powder	*1 teaspoon curry powder*
1 teaspoon dry mustard powder	*1 teaspoon dry mustard powder*
1 teaspoon tumeric	*1 teaspoon tumeric*
500 g sugar	*1 lb sugar*
500 ml malt or pickling vinegar	*1 pint malt or pickling vinegar*

Peel the marrow. Remove the seeds and cut up the flesh. Cut the cauliflower into sprigs. Cut up the cucumber (unpeeled). Peel and grate the carrots. Skin and finely chop the onions. Place the vegetables in a large pan, sprinkle with salt and cover with water. Leave overnight. The next day, drain the vegetables, removing as much liquid as possible.

Sauce: Mix the flour and spices together. Add 2 tablespoons of the vinegar and make into a smooth paste. Add the remaining vinegar, stirring to prevent the formation of lumps. Heat gently until the sauce thickens. Add the drained vegetables to the sauce. Mix well and cook through for 5 minutes. Cool and pot in sterilized jars. Close and leave for 1 month before using.

CONFECTIONERY - MELYSFWYD

TREACLE TOFFEE - TAFFI TRIOG

METRIC
400 g demerara sugar
125 ml water
75 g butter
100 g black treacle
100 g golden syrup
pinch cream of tartar

IMPERIAL
1 lb demerara sugar
¼ pint water
3 oz butter
4 oz black treacle
4 oz golden syrup
pinch cream of tartar

Heat the sugar in the water in a heavy based saucepan until the sugar has dissolved. Add the remaining ingredients and boil to 132°C, 270°F (soft crack stage). Pour into a 17 cm (7 inch) tin that has been greased with butter. Cool for 5 minutes then mark into squares with a knife. Leave to set. When cold, break into pieces. (Soft crack stage: drop ¼ teaspoon toffee syrup into a cup of cold water and work it with your fingers. Hard separate threads form that bend when removed from the water.)

TOFFEE APPLES - AFALAU TAFFI

METRIC
8 apples
400 g sugar
125 ml water
2 teaspoons vinegar
pinch cream of tartar
red vegetable colouring (optional)

IMPERIAL
8 apples
1 lb sugar
¼ pint water
2 teaspoons vinegar
pinch cream of tartar
red vegetable colouring (optional)

Place sugar, water, vinegar and cream of tartar in a heavy based, deep saucepan. Stir and heat gently until the sugar has dissolved then boil rapidly for 15 minutes until the temperature is 150ºC, 300ºF (hard crack stage). Remove from the heat and add vegetable colouring. Push a wooden skewer through each apple and dip apples in the syrup until coated. Place on a greased baking tray until hard. If the toffee starts to set in the pan, gently heat it again. (Hard crack stage: drop ¼ teaspoon toffee syrup into a cup of cold water and work it with your fingers. Brittle threads form that remain brittle when removed from the water.)

CREAMY FUDGE - CYFFUG HUFENNOG

METRIC
400 g sugar
2 tablespoons golden syrup
75 g butter
125 ml milk
¼ teaspoon vanilla flavouring

IMPERIAL
1 lb sugar
2 tablespoons golden syrup
3 oz butter
¼ pint milk
¼ teaspoon vanilla flavouring

Place the sugar, butter and milk into a heavy based saucepan. Heat gently and stir until the sugar dissolves. Bring to the boil and boil without stirring until the temperature is 116ºC, 240ºF (the soft ball stage), stirring occasionally to prevent sticking. Remove the pan from the heat, add the vanilla flavouring and beat with a wooden spoon until the mixture is thick and grainy. Pour into an 18 cm (7 inch) shallow square tin that has been greased with butter and leave for 5 - 10 minutes until almost set. Mark into squares with a knife and leave to cool. Break into squares. (Soft ball stage: drop ¼ teaspoon mixture into a cup of cold water and a soft ball is formed.)

CHOCOLATE FUDGE - CYFFUG SIOCLED

Break 75 g (3 oz) plain chocolate into pieces and melt in a basin standing over hot water. Add with the sugar, butter and milk as in the recipe for fudge.

HONEY FUDGE - CYFFUG MÊL

Add 2 tablespoons honey to the sugar, butter and milk in the recipe for fudge.

NUT FUDGE - CYFFUG CNAU

Add 2 tablespoons chopped nuts to the sugar, butter and milk in the recipe for fudge.

RUM TRUFFLES - TRYFFLS RWM

METRIC
100 g plain chocolate
50 g caster sugar
50 g cake crumbs
2 tablespoons rum (or sherry)
2 tablespoons apricot jam
50 g chocolate vermicelli

IMPERIAL
4 oz plain chocolate
2 oz caster sugar
2 oz cake crumbs
2 tablespoons rum (or sherry)
2 tablespoons apricot jam
2 oz chocolate vermicelli

Soak the cake crumbs in rum or sherry. Break the chocolate into pieces and melt in a basin standing over hot water. Remove from the heat and beat in the sugar and cake crumbs. When cool, form into balls, coat with apricot jam and vermicelli. Leave until firm and pack in sweet cases.

DRINKS - DIODYDD

MULLED WINE - GWIN POETH

METRIC
600 ml port or claret
300 ml water
75 g sugar
pinch each cinnamon, ginger and nutmeg
juice of ¼ lemon

IMPERIAL
1 pint port or claret
½ pint water
3 oz sugar
pinch each cinnamon, ginger and nutmeg
juice of ¼ lemon

Mix all the ingredients together except the port or claret and boil. Add the wine and heat but do not boil. Serve hot.

GINGER BEER - DIOD SINSIR

METRIC
25 g bruised ginger
2 lemons
15 g cream of tartar
500 g sugar
15 g yeast
1 slice of toast
4 litres water

IMPERIAL
1 oz bruised ginger
2 lemons
½ oz cream of tartar
1 lb sugar
½ oz yeast
1 slice of toast
8 pints water

Grate the rinds of the lemons and boil with the ginger, cream and sugar. Pour into a large bowl and add the rest of the water. Spread the yeast on the toast and float on top of the liquid. Cover with a cloth and leave for 24 hours. Strain and bottle. Cork loosely. Leave for 2 or 3 days.

MEAD - MEDD

METRIC	IMPERIAL
15 g yeast	*¼ oz yeast*
1 slice of bread, toasted	*1 slice of bread, toasted*
1 litre water	*2 pints water*
500 ml honey	*1 pint honey*
200 g sugar	*8 oz sugar*
1 lemon	*1 lemon*
few cloves	*few cloves*
piece of root ginger	*piece of root ginger*

Boil the honey and sugar in the water. Pour into a jar, removing any scum from the surface. Grate the ginger. Squeeze the lemon and strain the juice. Add the ginger and lemon juice and leave to cool. Spread the yeast on the bread. While the liquid is still warm, float the bread and yeast on the surface. Cover with a cloth or close loosely and leave for a week. Strain and bottle. Cork loosely and leave for 5 - 6 months.

FRUIT PUNCH - PWNSH FFRWYTHAU

METRIC	IMPERIAL
500 g mixed fruits - strawberries, raspberries, grapes, oranges, apples	1 lb mixed fruits - strawberries, raspberries, grapes, oranges, apples
500 ml unsweetened apple juice	1 pint unsweetened apple juice
500 ml orange juice	1 pint orange juice
500 ml lemonade	1 pint lemonade

Wash the fruit, peel and slice if necessary. Put the fruit into a large bowl and add the liquids. Stir. Serve decorated with slices of orange or lemon.

INDEX - MYNEGAI

Bacon pie - Pastai cig moch, 24
Baked trout - Brithyll pob, 22
Banana and honey teabread - Torth de banana a mel, 31
Bidding pie - Pastai neithior, 23
Bread and butter pudding - Pwdin bara menyn, 36
Buck rarebit - Caws pob a wy, 12

Caerphilly pudding - Pwdin Caerffili, 14
Cakes - Teisennau, 29
Chicken and leek soup - Cawl cyw iâr a chennin, 8
Chicken stock - Isgell cyw iâr, 27
Chocolate creams - Pwdin siocled hufennog, 38
Chocolate fudge - Cyffug siocled, 43
Chunky marmalade - Marmaled bras, 40
Cockle and bacon pie - Pastai cocos a chig moch, 19
Cockles Penclawdd - cocos Penclawdd, 18
Confectionery - Melysfwyd, 42
Country cake - Cacen ffrwythau cymysg, 29
Creamy fudge - Cyffug hufennog, 43
Currant bread - Bara brith, 32

Date and walnut loaf - Torth datys a chnau ffrengig, 32
Desserts - Pwdinau, 35
Drinks - Diodydd, 45

Eggs and leeks - wyau a chennin, 10
Eve's pudding - Pwdin Efa, 36

Faggots and peas - Ffagots a phys, 13
Fish - Pysgod, 17
Fish cakes - Teisennau pysgod, 22
Fisherman's pie - Pastai pysgotwr, 21
Fruit punch - Pwnsh ffrwythau, 46

Ginger beer - Diod sinsir, 45
Glamorgan sausages - Selsig Morgannwg, 14

Ham, leeks and cheese - Ham, cennin a chaws, 10
Harvest soup - Cawl cynhaeaf, 9
Honey cake - Cacen fêl, 30
Honey fudge - Cyffug mêl, 44
Honeyed Welsh lamb, Cig oen Cymreig a mêl, 27

Katt pie - Pastai Katt, 24

Laverbread and bacon - Bara lawr a chig moch, 11
Leek and potato soup - Cawl cennin a thatws, 7

INDEX - MYNEGAI continued

Marrow chutney - Shwtni marro, 41
Mead - Medd, 46
Meat - Cigoedd, 23
Mulled wine - Gwin poeth, 45

Nut fudge - Cyffug cnau, 44

Onion soup - Cawl nionod, 8
Onion tart - Tarten winwns, 16

Pheasant with port - Ffesant â phort, 26
Plate cake - Teisen lap, 33
Plum chutney - Shwtni eirin, 39
Pork and apple potato pie -
   Pastai porc, afal a thatws, 25
Potato cakes - Teisennau tatws, 15
Prawn pâté - Pâté corgimwch, 17
Preserves and jams - Cyffaith a jam, 39

Raspberry ice - Sorbet mafon, 37
Raspberry and rhubarb jam - Jam mafon a riwbob, 40
Rum truffles - Tryffls rwm, 44

Savoury dishes - Blasusfwyd, 10
Soups - Cawl, 7

Teifi salmon - Eog Teifi, 20
Toffee apples - Afalau taffi, 42
Treacle toffee - Taffi triog, 42
Trout with bacon - Brithyll a chig moch, 20

Watkin Wynne pudding - Pwdin Watcyn Wynne, 35
Welsh rarebit - Caws pob, 12
Welsh salt duck - Hwyaden hallt Gymreig, 28
Welsh cakes - Picau ar y maen, 34